Primer/Level One
(Prep/Grade 1)

CLASSIC MELODIES *from* GREAT BALLETS

for PIANO

for beginners of all ages

Compiled, arranged & edited by

John W. Schaum

FOREWORD

The Schaum "Classic Melodies" series arouses an appreciation of great music in the beginning student. At the very outset, the student can play melodies by the world's great composers, including symphonies, operas and ballets. Duet accompaniments are included for each melody. The ensemble experience with teacher, parent or friend provides valuable rhythmic training. All books have gummed award stamps. A music memory game for each book supplies valuable ear training experience.

The "Classic Melodies" series consists of the following four books:

- Classic Melodies from GREAT BALLETS
  Themes, illustrations & stories from 20 famous ballets
- Classic Melodies from GREAT COMPOSERS
  Representing 20 master composers from Bach to Bartok
- Classic Melodies from GREAT OPERAS
  Includes "Madam Butterfly", "La Boheme", "Pagliacci", "Carmen", "Aida"
- Classic Melodies from GREAT SYMPHONIES
  Excerpts from 20 symphonies by Beethoven, Haydn, Mozart, etc.

SCHAUM PUBLICATIONS, INC.
10235 N. Port Washington Rd. • Mequon, WI 53092
www.schaumpiano.net

07-41
I-16

contents

the 5 Basic Ballet Positions

1 2 3 4 5

Demi Plié

Knees bend out and heels do not leave the floor

Demi-Pointes

On the balls of the feet

Sur Les Pointes

On the tips of the toes

Point Tendue

Foot is stretched, toe is pointed

1. SWAN LAKE

A ballet is a dance which tells a story. "Swan Lake" tells of a prince on a hunting trip who is about to aim his crossbow at a swan. The Swan Queen appears and begs him not to shoot. The Swan Queen is really a beautiful maiden transformed into a swan by a magician. The prince falls in love with her and they dance together.

place ARABESQUE
stamp here

ARABESQUE (*ah-rah-BESK*) in dance means an Arabian design performed by the body. From basic position 5 (see title page for 5 basic positions) the back foot is carried back, toe is pointed, and knee is straight.

P. I. Tchaikowsky (1840-1893)

Maestoso

ACCOMPANIMENT

2. SPECTRE DE LA ROSE

A young girl returns home after a ball and falls asleep in her chair with a rose pressed to her lips. In her dreams, a spirit of youth garbed in rose petals leaps through her window and draws her into a dance; then he disappears into the night. The girl awakes and stoops to pick up the rose.

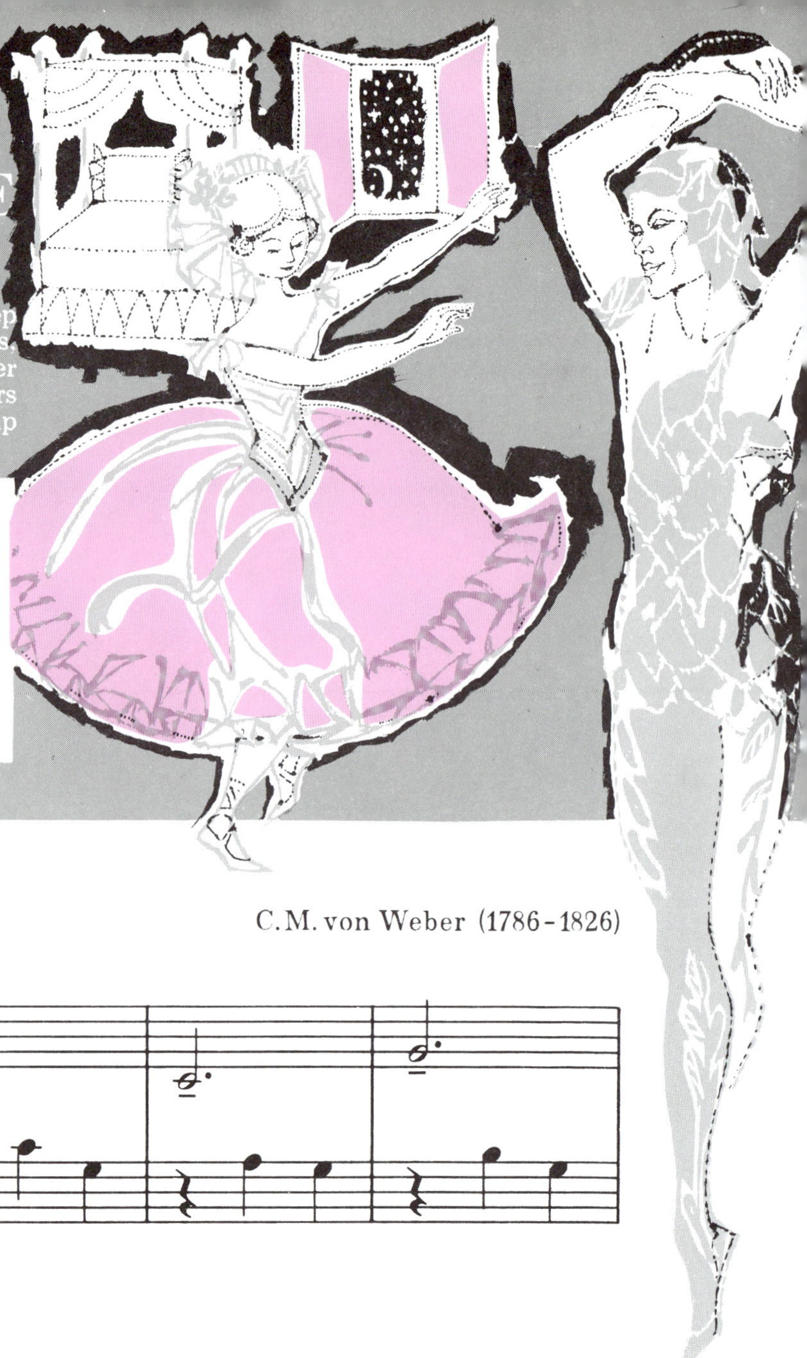

BOURREE (*boor-RAY*) is a repetitive step on demi-pointes or pointes, with knees turned out, covering ground in any direction.

place BOURRÉE stamp here

C.M. von Weber (1786-1826)

3. DANCE OF THE HOURS

The story is of a beautiful street singer named Giocanda (*joe-KAHN-dah*) who spurns the attentions of a spy. The spy accuses her mother of witchcraft. The mother is saved by a nobleman and there is a great dance in the palace. Black dancers, representing night, are overcome by colorful dancers who represent day. The "Dance of the Hours" marks the triumph of good over evil.

place JETÉ stamp here

JETÉ (*zheh-TAY*) means "to throw". The dancer jumps into the air and the weight is transferred from one foot to the other.

Allegro A. Ponchielli (1834 - 1886)

ACCOMPANIMENT

4. SLEEPING BEAUTY

"Sleeping Beauty" is the story of a princess who has been cursed by a wicked fairy. She must sleep 100 years until Prince Charming comes and kisses her. The court then awakes to a great wedding.

place BALANCE´ stamp here

BALANCE´ (*baa-lahn-SAY*) is a waltz step (3/4 time).

P. I. Tchaikowsky (1840-1893)

Tempo di Valse

ACCOMPANIMENT

5. THE DYING SWAN

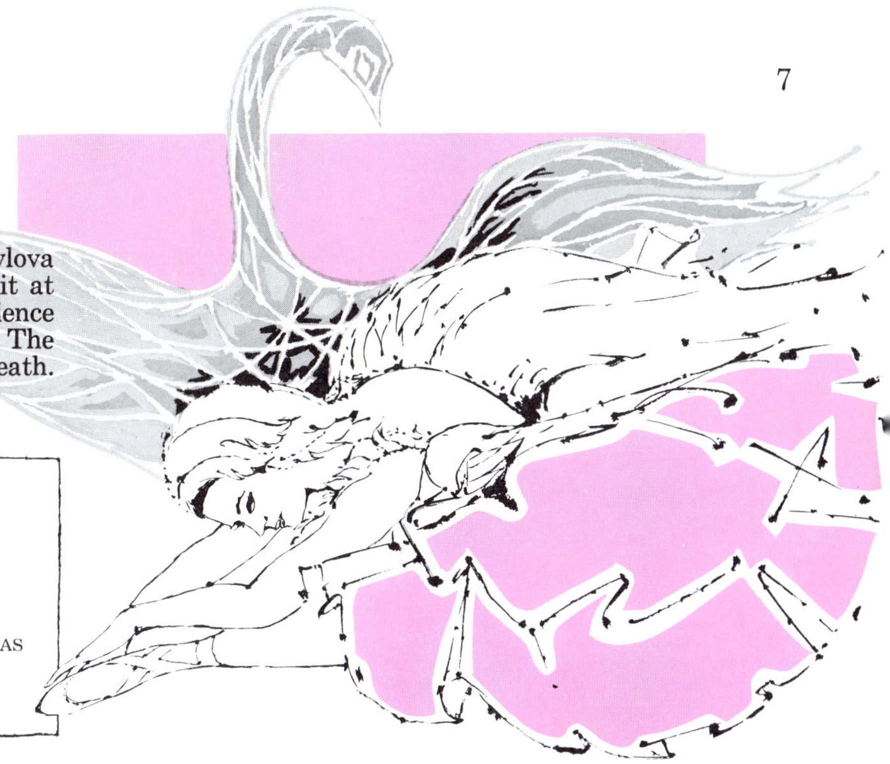

This dance was especially created for Anna Pavlova (*pah-VLOVE-ah*), the great ballerina. She danced it at a charity program in St. Petersburg and the audience liked it so well, she included it in her many tours. The dance tells the story of a swan's struggle against death.

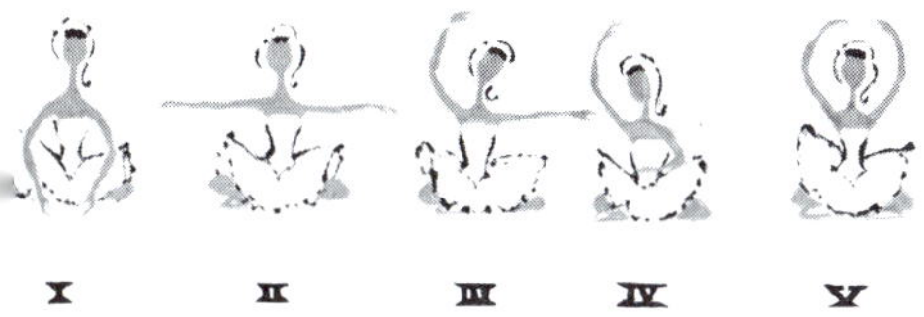

PORT DE BRAS (*pord' BRAH*) means "carriage of the arms". Shown above are the 5 basic arm positions.

place PORT DE BRAS stamp here

C. Saint-Saens (1835-1921)

ACCOMPANIMENT

6. GAÎTÉ PARISIENNE

Gaîté Parisienne (*gay-TAY peh-ree-ZYEN*) is a story about a tourist from Peru with two carpet bags full of money, who tries to crash society in a Paris cafe. There are soldiers, can-can dancers and an enchanting glove merchant who flirts with him.

PAS DE CHEVAL (*pahd' SHVAL*) is a prance. In French it means "horse step". From position 5 with knees well out, plié, lifting one knee high, point toe down and jump. Lift the other foot fast.

Jacques Offenbach (1819-1880)

ACCOMPANIMENT

7. LES SYLPHIDES

Les Sylphides (*lay sill-FEEDS*) is a ballet without a story. Into a moonlight glade come the dancers, pure white sylphs (*sillfs*) with long skirts. Sylphs are graceful fairy maidens. They are joined by a single male in black doublet and white tights. At the end, the airy phantoms all fade away.

GRAND JETÉ (*grahn zheh-TAY*) means "big throw" or high leap. Point toe forward, then a run and leap to perform a split in mid-air, land in demi-plié in arabesque position.

Tempo di Valse

F. Chopin (1810-1849)

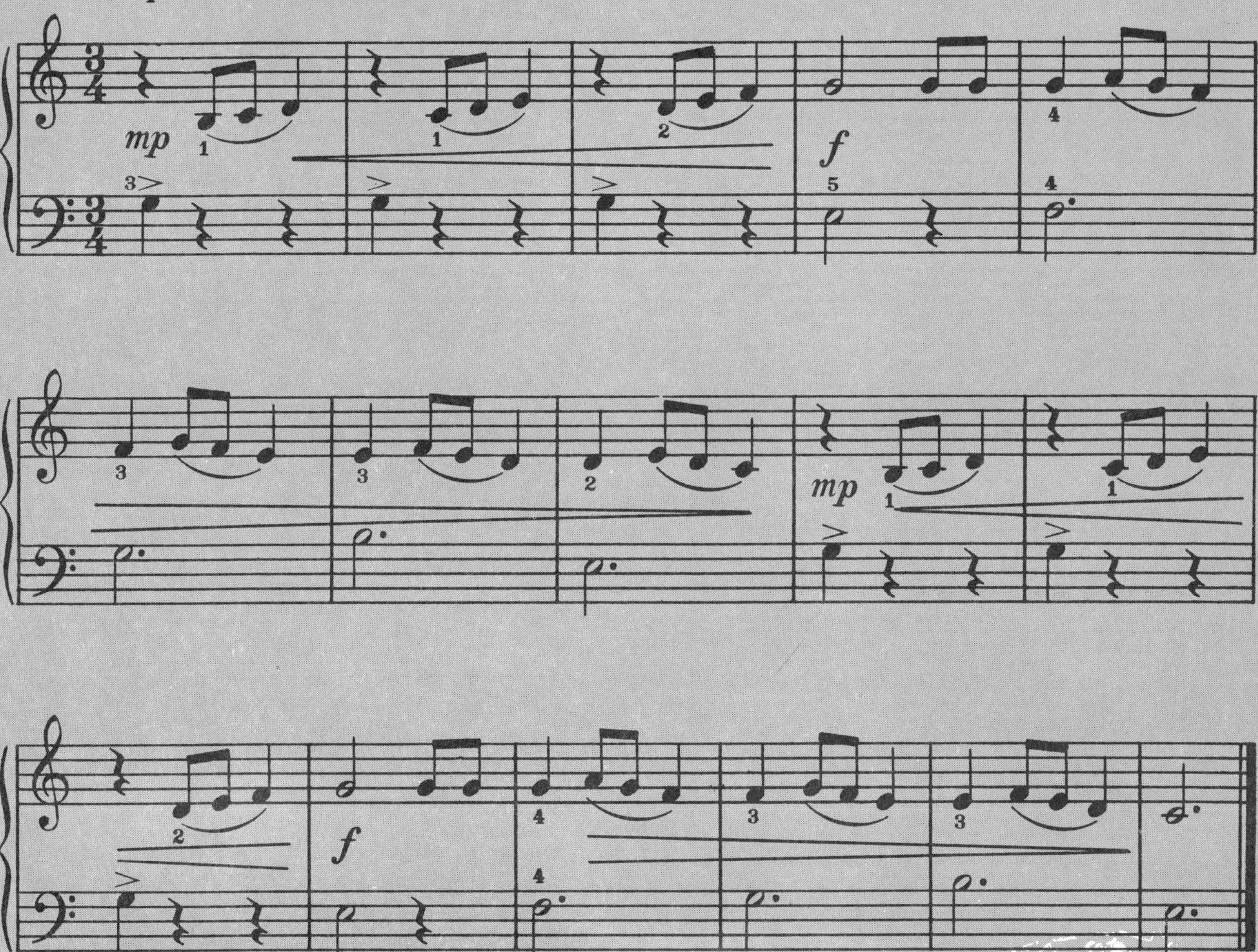

ACCOMPANIMENT

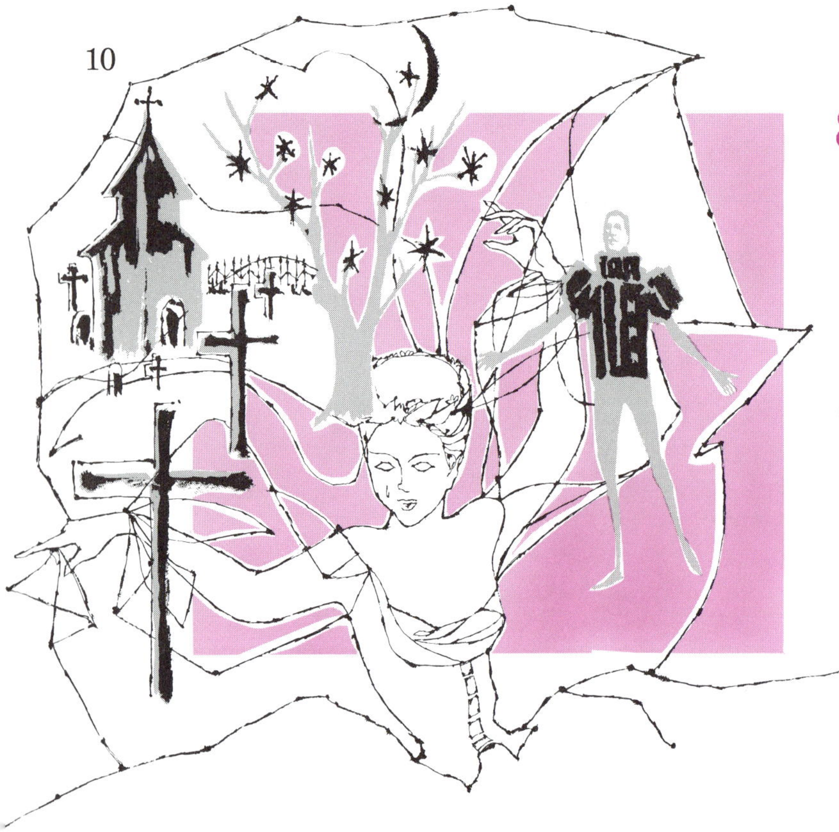

8. GISELLE

Giselle (*ji-ZELL*) is a village girl who is courted by a prince disguised as a peasant. When she discovers her lover is of noble blood, she dances herself to death in a fit of madness. In the grave, she joins the ghosts of maidens who died before their wedding day. The prince visits her tomb and, seized with the fatal dance madness, collapses over her grave.

place GLISSADE ATTITUDE stamp here

GLISSADE ATTITUDE (*glee-SAHD ah-tee-TEWD*) means a gliding movement into a specific pose. We show here the front attitude.

Adolphe Adam (1803-1856)

Lento

ACCOMPANIMENT

9. PETER AND THE WOLF

Peter has three friends: a bird, a duck, and a cat. In an adventure in the woods, the duck is eaten by a wicked wolf. Peter with the help of the cat and the bird captures the wolf and triumphantly marches him to the zoo.

PAS DE BOURRÉE (*pahd' boor-RAY*) is a complex series of little steps on demi-pointes or pointes, in which the feet weave in and out.

place PAS DE BOURRÉE stamp here

Andantino
(See Footnote)

Serge Prokofieff (1891-1953)

ACCOMPANIMENT

TEACHER'S NOTE: If the pupil is in the early grades in school and has not had fractions, do not attempt to explain the dotted quarter notes and rests. The rule to follow is this: EXPERIENCE SHOULD PRECEDE EXPLANATION. Teach the rhythm by rote. Delay the explanation until the problem arises at a later time when the pupil has acquired fraction readiness.

10. TILL EULENSPIEGEL

Till Eulenspiegel (*OY-len-shpee-gel*) was a wandering Jack-of-all-trades who journeyed through the country-side playing tricks on everyone he met. His mischievous jokes made him many enemies and finally brought disaster to him.

place CHAÎNE-TOUR stamp here

CHAÎNE-TOUR (*sheh-nay TOOR*) is a chain of turns, a series of small steps on demi-pointes or pointes.

Moderato

Richard Strauss (1864-1949)

ACCOMPANIMENT

11. DANCE OF THE COMEDIANS

Comedians (*kah-ME-dee-ans*) are actors who play comic parts. The ballet takes place in a village market place where a small circus is preparing to perform. The clowns, acrobats, jugglers, and other merrymakers join in the gay "Dance of the Comedians".

TEMPS LEVE´ (*tahn leh-VAY*), a timed jump, is started from any of the 5 positions, demi-plie´. The dancer jumps straight up, toes well pointed, and lands back in the starting position.

Bedrich Smetana (1824-1884)

Allegretto

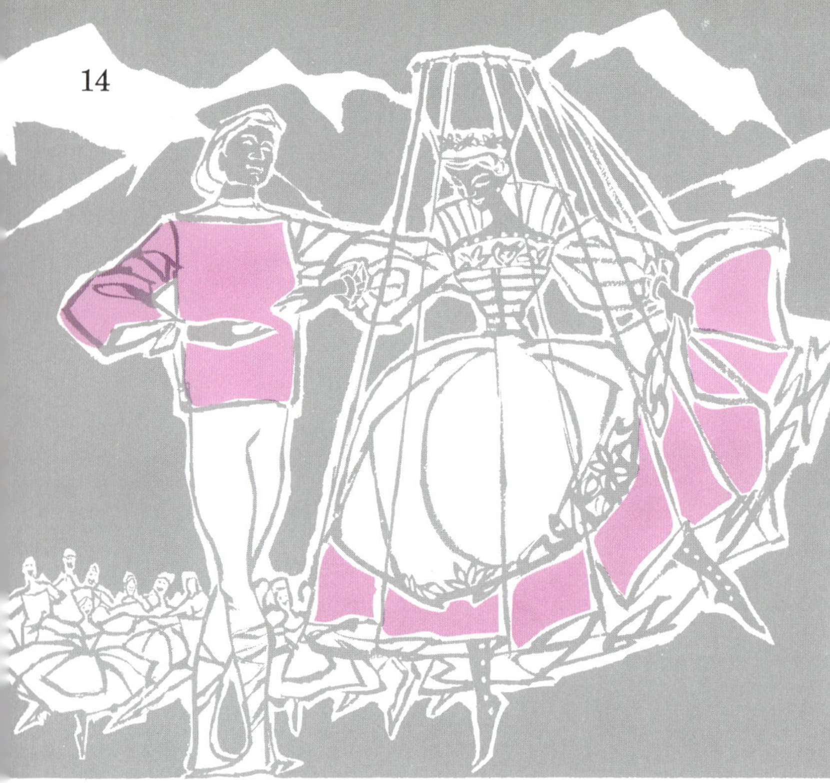

12. WEDDING DANCE

The music is from the opera William Tell. This story has become very famous, especially the part where Tell is forced to shoot an apple off his son's head. The "Wedding Dance" is performed to celebrate the marriage of a commoner to the daughter of the dictator, Gessler.

place GLISSADE stamp here

GLISSADE (*glee-SAHD*) is a gliding step. From position 5 the back foot moves into second position. The weight then is put on it, and the other foot draws forward into position 5 again and plié. We are showing the front glissade.

G. Rossini (1792-1868)

Andantino

ACCOMPANIMENT

13. THE MIKADO

The comic opera Mikado (*mi-KAH-doe*) has been made into a ballet. The name Mikado refers to the ruler of Japan. One of the delightful parts is the tantrum of a court gentleman who must marry the unattractive daughter-in-law-elect of the Mikado.

ASSEMBLÉ (*ah-sahm-BLAY*) means "bring together". From position 5 brush the back foot out, jump into the air, descend to position 5 and plié— both feet landing at the same time.

place ASSEMBLÉ stamp here

Sir William Gilbert (1836-1911) | Sir Arthur Sullivan (1842-1900)

Allegretto

ACCOMPANIMENT

14. ROSAMUNDE

The play Rosamunde by von Chezy includes the famous ballet music by Franz Schubert. The story is about a shepherdess who is informed that she is really a princess and that the ruler wishes to marry her. Because she declines to marry him, the ruler sends her a poisoned letter. She does not read it and it is returned to him. The ruler's wickedness destroys him.

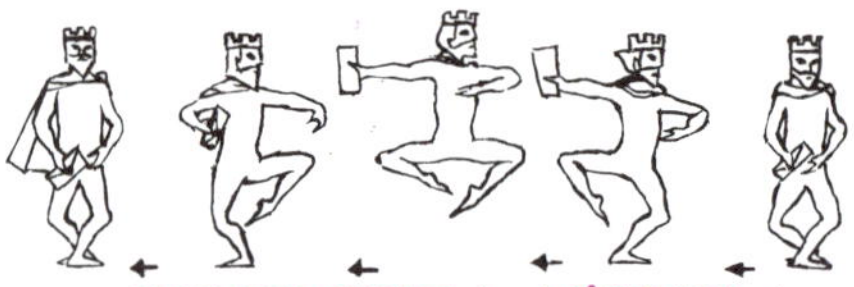

PAS DE CHAT (*pahd'SHAH*) translates "cat step". From position 5 the toe of the back foot rises to the knee of the other leg and springs down while the other foot rises and goes back in front. Both feet are off the ground for a moment; then the dancer lands in position 5 plie, and repeats.

place PAS DE CHAT stamp here

F. Schubert (1797-1828)

Allegro

ACCOMPANIMENT

15. COPPÉLIA

Coppélia (*Ko-PAIL-yah*) is a beautiful life-size mechanical doll. Swanilda, a village girl, is shocked when she discovers that her boy friend appears to be in love with Coppélia. Swanilda breaks into the doll factory and dresses in the doll's clothes. She winds up the other dolls and has them create a terrible rumpus. The confused boy friend is straightened out and everything ends happily.

place GRAND PLIE stamp here

GRAND PLIÉ (*grahn plee-AY*) means "big bend". In position 1 or any of the 5 positions, the knees bend out to the side as far as they will go. Heels rise off the floor as the dancer lowers herself.

Leo Delibes (1836-1891)

Maestoso

ACCOMPANIMENT

16. PETROUCHKA

Petrouchka (*pe-TROOSH-kah*) is a ballet about a puppet show. The main dancers are three puppets in a carnival booth. The clown, Petrouchka, is in love with the ballerina, but she loves the Moor, and the Moor kills the clown. Spectators complain, police come, but the puppeteer says the clown is only sawdust. The police leave, but from above is heard a horrible scream from the ghost of Petrouchka.

CHANGEMENT (*shahn - ZHMAW*) means "change". The dancer jumps in the air from position 5, back foot changes to front, and dancer lands in position 5.

place CHANGEMENT stamp here

Igor Stravinsky (1882-1971)

Allegro

ACCOMPANIMENT

17. THE NUTCRACKER

Late at night a little girl finds a battle going on around the Christmas tree. The tin soldiers, led by the magic nutcracker, are fighting mice. The girl hits the king mouse over the head with her slipper and the nutcracker turns into a prince. He takes her to see the "Waltz of the Flowers" from which the following music comes.

TOUR JETÉ (*toor zheh-TAY*) means "turn and throw". The dancer makes a turn in mid-air and lands in arabesque position.

place TOUR JETÉ stamp here

P. I. Tchaikowsky (1840-1893)

Tempo di Valse

ACCOMPANIMENT

18. TAMBOURINE

The ballet music entitled "Tambourine" is all that has survived from a long forgotten opera by Grétry who was a founder of the school of French comic opera. His music is easily adaptable to the dance.

CHASSÉ (*shay-SAY*) is a step in which one foot pushes the other "chasing" it from position.

André Grétry (1742-1813)

ACCOMPANIMENT

19. SYLVIA

Sylvia, a woodland fairy, shoots an arrow at a statue of the god of love. The arrow misses the statue and accidentally wounds a shepherd. The statue comes to life and shoots Sylvia with a golden arrow which causes her to fall in love with the shepherd. A wicked hunter kidnaps her, but the god of love straightens it out, and it all ends happily.

place PIQUÉ stamp here

PIQUÉ (*pee-KAY*) means a "reach". One foot reaches to demi-pointe or pointe and the other foot is raised, knee turned out to the side, and placed just above the ankle of the first.

Leo Delibes (1836-1891)

Moderato

ACCOMPANIMENT

20. SCHEHEREZADE

Queen Scheherezade (*shah-hair-ah-ZAHD*) is the make-believe story-teller of the tales of the Arabian Nights. One of these stories is about a jealous sultan. To test the faithfulness of his wife he pretends to go on a hunting expedition. He returns unexpectedly and finds a wild party in progress. Tragedy and death bring the story to an unhappy ending.

RÉVÉRENCE (*ray-vay-RAHNSS*) is a curtsey. From position 5 the front foot slides to second position and the other foot moves behind it into fourth position. The knees bend out and the head is lowered. This is the ballerina's way of saying, "Thank you".

N. Rimsky-Korsakov (1844-1908)

ACCOMPANIMENT

THE SCHAUM MUSIC MEMORY GAME

(Great Ballets)

DIRECTIONS: Below are four-measure themes from each of the twenty pieces in this book. They are grouped in irregular order. You are to identify them by consulting the list and placing the correct number in each square. The first theme is Giselle, which is No. 8, therefore the number eight has been placed in the square.

1. Swan Lake
2. Spectre de la Rose
3. Dance of the Hours
4. Sleeping Beauty
5. The Dying Swan
6. Gaite Parisienne
7. Les Sylphides
8. Giselle
9. Peter and the Wolf
10. Till Eulenspiegel
11. Dance of the Comedians
12. Wedding Dance
13. The Mikado
14. Rosamunde
15. Coppelia
16. Petrouchka
17. The Nutcracker
18. Tambourine
19. Sylvia
20. Scheherezade

TEACHER'S NOTE: This game provides excellent ear training opportunity. Play the themes for the student and have him identify them. It can also be adapted to provide entertaining instruction for music clubs and recitals.

Successful Schaum Sheet Music

This is a Partial List — Showing Level 1 through Level 2

✋= 5 Finger Position * = Big Notes • = Original Form ✓ = Chord Symbols

ACTION SOLOS

LEVEL

52-07 *• ASTRONAUT ADVENTURE (L. H. Melody) *Schaum* 1
52-25 *• BUBBLE BLUES .... *Weston* 1
55-20 * POGO STICK CHOP (Based on "Chop Sticks") *Schaum* 2
55-34 • RIGHT ON (Staccato) .... *Miller* 2
55-26 • WATER SLIDE (Staccato) .... *Payne* 2

AMERICAN – PATRIOTIC SOLOS

55-14 AMERICA THE BEAUTIFUL .... *Ward* 2
55-41 MARINES' HYMN .... *Traditional* 2
55-08 WABASH CANNON BALL .... *Railroad Song* 2

ANIMALS and BIRDS

52-16 *• BUSY WOODPECKER ✋(Staccato) .... *Cahn* 1
52-36 • DINOSAUR LAND .... *Schaum* 1
55-54 • EQUESTRIAN PROCESSION .... *Cahn* 2
52-38 • KANGAROO HOP ✋ .... *Polk* 1
52-24 *• PERKY TURKEY .... *Weston* 1
55-09 *• POPPO the PORPOISE (L. H. Melody) ... *Littlewood* 2

BOOGIE

55-07 *• COOL SCHOOL (Boogie Style) .... *Schaum* 2
55-02 • LITTLE DOG BOOGIE .... *Schaum* 2

BOTH HANDS in TREBLE CLEF

52-27 • JOYOUS BELLS ✋ (with Duet Accomp.) .... *Cahn* 1
55-56 • MUSIC BOX LULLABY .... *Levin* 2
55-44 • MYSTICAL ETUDE (Staccato) .... *Cahn* 2

CHRISTMAS

70-10 * IT CAME UPON THE MIDNIGHT CLEAR .. *Trad.* 1
81-06 LITTLE DRUMMER BOY, The .... *Arr. Schaum* 1
81-07 SANTA CLAUS IS COMIN' TO TOWN *Arr. Schaum* 1
70-02 TWELVE DAYS of CHRISTMAS ...... *All 12 Verses* 1
70-01 * WHAT CHILD IS THIS? ("Greensleeves") .... *Trad.* 1

CIRCUS

55-39 • CIRCUS PONIES .... *Leach* 2
55-58 • CLOWN WALTZ .... *Kitchen* 2
55-53 • RINGMASTER'S MARCH .... *Cahn* 2

CLASSICS

52-09 * *Beethoven* . SONG of JOY ("Ode To Joy" from 9th Symph.) 1
52-37 *Grieg* ...... In the HALL of the MOUNTAIN KING 1
52-12 ✓ *Handel* .... HALLELUJAH CHORUS (Easy Edition) 1
55-30 *Mozart* MOZART'S ROMANCE ("A Little Night Music") 2
55-45 *Pachelbel* .... PACHELBEL'S CANON (Easy Edition) 2
52-35 *Rossini* .... WILLIAM TELL MARCH 1

COUNTRY/WESTERN

55-35 DAGGER DANCE ("Land of Sky Blue Waters") ... *Herbert* 2
52-06 *• PONY RIDE ✋ .... *McCreary* 1

DESCRIPTIVE MUSIC

52-39 • ANCIENT PAGODA .... *Biel* 1
52-43 *• BE A STAR ✋ .... *Rita* 1
55-46 COME BACK TO SORRENTO .... *deCurtis* 2
55-47 • DOMINOES .... *Cahn* 2
52-32 *• GLIDING ON THE WIND .... *Hampton* 1
52-44 *• GOING BY, MERRILY .... *Rita* 1
55-49 • IN A FAR OFF TIME & PLACE .... *Revezoulis* 2
52-42 *• IT'S FUN TO LEARN ✋ .... *Rita* 1
52-40 • JOLLY LEPRECHAUN .... *Revezoulis* 1
52-46 • JUST IMAGINE IT .... *Rita* 1
55-51 • PEACEFUL INTERLUDE .... *Holmes* 2
55-42 • SUNSET SERENADE .... *Levin* 2

DUET (1 Piano, 4 Hands)

LEVEL

71-02 PARADE of the TOY SOLDIERS .... *Jessel* 1
71-07 HARK the HERALD ANGELS SING ... *Traditional* 2

FOOD

55-38 • HURRY, LITTLE PIZZA CAR .... *Holmes* 2

HALLOWEEN

55-40 *• GALLOPING GHOSTS (Minor Key) *Weston/Schaum* 2
55-57 *• TRICK OR TREAT PARADE .... *Rita* 2
52-15 *• SPOOK HOUSE (L. H. Melody) .... *Schaum* 1
52-20 *• SPUNKY SPOOKS (Both Hands in Bass) .... *Weston* 1

JAZZ STYLE

55-48 • DUDE .... *Weston* 2

LEFT HAND MELODY

52-22 • KNOCKING AT MY DOOR ✋ .... *Schaum* 1
55-50 • SCOTTISH SKETCH .... *Holmes* 2

MARCHES

52-34 • FANFARE .... *King* 1
55-06 PARADE of the TOY SOLDIERS .... *Jessel* 2

MINOR KEY

55-52• DREAM CATCHER .... *Holmes* 2
52-28 • SECRET AGENT .... *Weston* 1

MOVIE THEME

80-01 STAR WARS (Main Title) .... *Williams* 2

OLDIES but GOODIES

52-21 ✓ SCHOOL DAYS .... *Edwards* 1

RAGTIME

55-21 *✓ENTERTAINER (Easy Version) .... *Joplin* 2
55-55 • RICKETY RAG .... *Schaum* 2

SACRED

55-25 *✓HOW GREAT THOU ART ..... *Swedish Folk Melody* 2

SPORTS

52-10 *• CHEERLEADER .... *Plank* 1
52-45 *• DAD'S DUNE BUGGY .... *Turner* 1
52-18 *• JOGGING TRAIL ✋ (Minor Key) .... *Payne* 1
55-43 • ROLLER BLADES .... *Schaum* 2
52-41 • SKI TRAILS .... *King* 1
55-28 ✓ TAKE ME OUT TO THE BALL GAME . *Von Tilzer* 2

SPRINGTIME

55-18 *• FAWN'S LULLABY .... *Masson* 2
52-04 * SPRING, SWEET SPRING .... *Lincke* 1
52-31 *• TREES IN THE BREEZE .... *Hampton* 1

STACCATO

55-23 *• FRISKY FROG (Both Hands in Treble) .... *Cahn* 2
52-33 • HOPSCOTCH .... *Hampton* 1
52-11 *• WINDSHIELD WIPER ROCK (Staccato) ...... *Noblitt* 1

THANKSGIVING

52-24 *• PERKY TURKEY .... *Weston* 1
55-12 THANKSGIVING SCENE .. *Medley of 4 Hymns* 2

WALTZES

52-30 • OPUS ONE .... *Cahn* 1